The Heart Whisperer

Hosain Mosavat

The Heart Whisperer

This book is written to provide information and motivation to readers. Its purpose is not to render any type of psychological, legal, or professional advice of any kind. The content is the sole opinion and expression of the author, and not necessarily that of the publisher.

Front cover by Judy Mosavat
Back cover by Hosain Mosavat
Calligraphy of Hosain Mosavat's name by Aydin Cayir

Copyright © 2019 by Hosain Mosavat

All rights reserved. No part of this book may be reproduced, transmitted, or distributed in any form by any means, including, but not limited to, recording, photocopying, or taking screenshots of parts of the book, without prior written permission from the author or the publisher. Brief quotations for noncommercial purposes, such as book reviews, permitted by Fair Use of the U.S. Copyright Law, are allowed without written permissions, as long as such quotations do not cause damage to the book's commercial value. For permissions, write to the publisher, whose address is stated below.

Printed in the United States of America.

ISBN   978-1-64552-001-6   (Paperback)
ISBN   978-1-64552-002-3   (Digital)

Lettra Press books may be ordered through booksellers or by contacting:

Lettra Press LLC
18229 E 52nd Ave.
Denver City, CO 80249
1 303 586 1431 | info@lettrapress.com
www.lettrapress.com

The Heart Whisperer

Hosain Mosavat

Contents

A Taste of My Existence 13
Acknowledgment 19
A Message from My Wife 21

The Poems
You wear more 23
If you've got a heart 25
Let us pour our hearts 27
A morning breeze 29
Today bring me food 31
When your heart beats like thunder 33
The fire is on 35
Like two candles 37
A rose 39
To show the richness 41
What did you see? 43
Love is the oxygen 45
Dew drops 47
You took too long to paint a rose 49
It doesn't take time 51
I want to learn no more 53
The more I am with the ocean 55
Be like grains of salt 57
Be still 59
I cannot explain 61
Come and celebrate 63
Love is a Spring breeze 65
Watching the Moon 67

The freshness of life	69
I told my secret	71
I am looking at the sunset	73
A darvish	75
Work on your own story	77
God gave us flowers	79
A songbird	81
Can you put half of your heart	83
Tonight let us taste devotion	85
Speak poetry	87
Meet me after midnight	89
Dance near me	91
Like a drop of rain	93
Take me with you	95
When love opens me up	97
Some doors	99
When I heard you coming	101
All who know	103
A Sufi is a swan	105
Only in silence	107
A thousand eyes	109
Love is a shock wave	111
Let us be clear	113
As far as I am concerned	115
Lover is that one	117
One night	119
When you plant a seed of love	121
When you are gone	123
How can I walk away	125
You pull one strand	127
Poetry	129
God will be happier	131
There is a light within us	133
Walk with your heart	135

It is about being beautiful	137
Practice revealing yourself like a rose	139
Gathering fragrant blossoms	141
When will you know the truth?	143
I love the wind	145
I saw you today	147
I am an ocean	149
At last	151
I put you in my hand	153
This soul will disappear	155
Lately my friendships have been limited	157
When I am quiet	159
The magic of love	161
As the sun sets	163
Looked at the universe	165
With such a small heart	167
Beneath my feet	169
The only thing	171
I was going homeward	172
Do not ask my lips	175
Keep arriving	177
When you come knocking	179
From a single cell	181
Who I am	183
I may be old	185
Like a migrating bird	187
A sunset is a promise	189
The day they created fire	191
You will never find me	193
Those were the days	195
Let me stay a little longer	197
Who knows where the time goes	199
If there is anything to be	201

A Taste Of My Existence

I was born in Shiraz, Iran ~ the land of roses, poets and Shiraz wine. So, I was sentenced to be a poet for the rest of my life. As I grew up, I met my true teacher, my Mother. She was the same Mother who sang poetry to put me to sleep and who later on taught me to create poetry, music, calligraphy and painting. From then on, I wanted to be a poet, a musician, a calligrapher and a painter, and everything else I could put my heart into. She taught me that I could do anything if I wanted it badly enough. When I was old enough to hold a Persian instrument called 'tar,' she taught me how to play it. I later became an accomplished tar player. And when I got older yet, she taught me painting. I became a photographer as a result. I woke up at almost 30 years of age to realize the seed of poetry she had planted in me. And writing heartfelt poetry became a part of my everyday existence. So far, I have written around 26,000 poems.

I went to school in Tehran and graduated from High School there. Two years before my graduation, the first Revolution in Iran began. The violence was great. The loss of many friends made me feel unwelcome in my own country without freedom. My father decided to send me to America, where I stayed and became a citizen, finished my schooling, and then taught Physics and Math for 30 years. During this time, I began to write poetry. I played music and I photographed extensively, traveling wherever it was possible and photographing as many places as I could physically go to. And all winter I developed and printed those images. I started with a Minnox camera, which has a half of a thumbnail-sized negative, to a 35 mm camera, to an 8"x10" View Camera, back down to 5"x7", because I couldn't carry that much weight any longer. And now I am totally digital.

I married 3 times, one son from the first wife, no fruits from the second wife and, finally, my third wife, Judy, became the love of my life, the friend I had been looking for. She began to travel with me, carry my tripod, then carry my camera, then complain, then convince me that I should reduce the size of my camera equipment to match my age and my physical ability. And now she carries her own digital camera, her own tripod, and stands in front of my camera to take her own pictures. What a joy to see her development.

When I first witnessed the digital world, I fell in love out of necessity for its lightness and portability, which saved Judy from being my private sherpa, and which, once again, got us on the road. Nowadays, with the extensive advance of digital cameras and inkjet printers, I am in heaven. I think digital can actually do better than any film photography. For this belief, I was almost thrown out of our Camera Club. But I persevered.

I retired from teaching in 1993 and am living in Whitmore Lake, Michigan. I've taken Judy to Iran twice, Germany, China, India, Turkey, and all states and Canada many times. I've taken over 30,000 images of Iran and have shown them to clubs, family and friends, and to fund-raising events for a good cause. And about a photography book, forget it. What I have put Judy through with even the first poetry book, if I mention a book of photography, she would surely put me in the doghouse, and that is not where I want to be. It's too cold in the winter, and not photogenic in the summer.

About my religion, I was raised as a Moslem and witnessed a few Sufis around my Father. I believe my Mother was a Sufi, but I didn't know it. As I learned more and more about religions in general, what people stood for and what they were against, they did not make any godly sense to me. So I began to free myself from beliefs and naturally fell into Sufism. They believe either I am nothing or I am everything. I'm not a Jew nor a Moslem nor a Christian. I'm not a Hindu, Buddhist nor a Zoroastrian. Therefore, I make no distinction between them, and I accept them all at once. That makes me everything. Therefore, I am a Jew, a Moslem and a Christian, and every other belief that exists. Yet I do not exist as any of them. I am an image of the creation with one heart. And within that one heart exists a universal love.

As far as my age, I was born in 1934. That makes me 79 years old at this time. I don't plan to live long. I plan to live one day at a time. No, let me amend that. I plan to live one breath at a time.

My hobbies have been photography, computers, traveling, poetry, music, woodturning, welding, cooking, friendship and laughing. I try to be funny when I'm not. I try to bring laughter to any tears. And I don't really care how crazy I am, as long as I bring laughter every chance I get.

When I came to this country, I had lost many friends of mine in the Revolution. I did not speak English. As a result, I did not have many friends. Going to school was my only contact with people. When I would get back to my dorm room and finish my homework, I would cry of loneliness. I remember once I wrote a letter to my Father, and when I finished it, some of the words on the paper were smeared. I realized it was my fallen tears. No one could understand my tears better than I. So I began to write extensive letters of feelings to the friends and family I left behind. And when I learned English well enough and had left everything behind so I could survive in this country, I had a lot to say. So I began to write poetry in English, however the language was limiting to me. But I was able to relay the feelings. After two broken marriages, a son that I abandoned and a few broken relationships, I began to write emotional poetry. And when I shared it with friends, they encouraged me to write a book, write more and share more. Although I had everything I needed to continue, I needed these friends to keep me going, to light my fire, and let me burn in love instead of anger and loneliness.

Then I met Judy, my last and only wife, and she became the backbone of my creativity. This is where the first book came from. She inspired it, typed it, chased publishers, begged friends and borrowed to make the first book. And that was not the last of it. She has now brought forth two more. I will always be grateful to her.

Each poem in my books is an image of a living moment in my life. Life as you live it has infinite phrases, poetry, music, colors, songs, sadnesses, happinesses, births and deaths. And a book of life has infinite chapters and a complete universe of feelings. I can only share a few winks at a time. So enjoy these books. Maybe the next book will be yours. If that happens, I am finished with poetry, for you will be writing my poetry coming out of your heart, which means we have become one.

Twice in my life, I almost died. For no reason at all, I survived. As I looked at my life in total, I'd done everything. Since then, these books have taken on lives of their own. I have written many more poems than even surprises me. Sometimes I have to rush out of the bathroom or get up in the middle of the night to write a poem. It is coming to me that the reason I am alive today is to share what I can offer. And that is, in fact, the very reason for any human being to be alive: to spread enduring love and care and to join for the safety of humanity, so that we can stand together as beacons of love. I am humbled to live among you, my dear ones. In oneness, we become one family of mankind. We can heal and be healed. We can sing, dance and be merry in any language. We need to be the eyes for those who are unable to see. We need to be the voices of people everywhere. This is our destiny. I live to see this.

Acknowledgment

My wife's name is Judy. The owner of my heart is Judy. All that I am proud of is Judy. The only companion that stood by me in two incidents of escaping the fangs of death is Judy. The only person who put me together and disciplined me in order to put these books together and forced me to sit down and listen to the selections of these poems is Judy. The one who chose the right poems to channel the right projection of my feelings is Judy. The one who fought with me to make my days brilliant and prepared me to read poetry is Judy. So who is this Judy? Is she someone to sleep with, eat with, argue with, fight for money with, decide who's the boss and who runs this little gathering called marriage? Judy is above all of that. She was there before I asked. She was present when I asked. She never fought back; instead loved me back. In the past, I have given her many names: friend, companion, lover, precious and, of course, in an instant of madness on my part, I have called her unmentionable names. She's a friend so close that at times every move she makes is my move. Sometimes we say things exactly the same at the same time. She has become so close to me, that I cannot separate her from me. In one word, she is us.

Hosain

You are a bird
whose sweet song purifies every listening heart

You are the sunrise
whose brilliant colors pull light from darkness

You are the breeze
a gentle hand to lift birds in flight

Keep singing the world into light and flight, Love

Keep singing

Judy

You wear more when you are naked
than when you are love

If you've got a heart
      and you're ready to offer it to the world
Then you better come

If you are ready
      and craving for touch
You better come
And together we'll touch the world

Between you and the world today
      every heartbeat in the world
           hungers for all the above
You no longer have the luxury of sitting home
      and leaving it to someone else
You better come

The sign of destruction is everywhere
It hasn't reached your home
      but it will
You better come

A little time of togetherness
      may just bring you some comfort and peace

My dear friends,
I don't have much time to go
You can see I'm just as desperate as you will be
      when you wake up
You better come

When you go home
      there is a world of care awaiting
You better come

Let us pour our hearts into a keg
Where we can blend with each other
      to brew wine
         and to make a general amnesty
            to all who get intoxicated with this wine

What harm would it do
      if a drunken heart takes over the world
         and says 'You're all free'

Everyone should drink from the same keg
      to become bewildered in love

Follow no direction except
      the oneness
         that tastes no taste but love

Let us brew such wine
      by standing for peace
      and saying 'I love you'
And together saying 'We love us'

A morning breeze came to visit
My heart was out the door before me
When this trio got together
    morning breeze, my heart and me
It was heaven on earth

Soon after
    the sun rose to give us light and warmth
Only then
I realized how hungry I was
    to see love pouring out of me
No more sickness or danger could touch me

Come
Gather around
I have something to share

Today bring me food
> not scalded in boiling water
> or charred on a skewer

Something sweetened in burning love
Something that has passed through
> the breath of peace
Something so cool
> that it brings with it earth-shaking reality

Yes
Bring me a plate of truth
That is the food I have hungered for
> for so long

When your heart beats like thunder
And you speak like lightening
And your sword cuts through the veils

Then you have arrived to do battle for love

The fire is on
Laughter is in flame
Both of us are intoxicated
    this rose and me
In our silence
    we burn hotter than fire
    dance faster than any flame

Come and watch me
    as I disappear into the hearts of those
    who are the dance and the dancer
        lover and Beloved

When we learn to dance within each other
    separation no longer exists
Lover and Beloved are at their best
    and all have reached onehood

Dance! . . . if you have the courage
Dance! . . . if you ever wish to love
Dance! . . . if you wish to be peace
Dance! . . . to understand life
Dance! . . .
Dance! . . .
Dance! . . .

Like two candles
      rushing to make the same flame

Like the ocean waves
      rushing to meet the shores

Like waterfalls free-falling
      to resemble the naked power of beauty

Like a songbird saying
      'I am singing my heart out for you'

Like night
      rushing to meet the sun
           to give birth to a new day

Tell me
Is this not a tapestry of love
      which is our home?

A rose
> without introduction
>> opens to a butterfly

And a butterfly
> without permission
>> sits at the heart of a rose

Such beauties are never questioned

Tell me
Why can't a man's heart be like a rose?
Why can't a man's spirit be like a butterfly?

To show the richness of white light
    all the colors of the spectrum must be present

To show the richness of life
    the whole of humanity must be dignified

What did you see?
What is this giving up?
Your tears are so big
      they are drowning your future

Come back ~
There is another way of looking at things

Freedom
      is the deepest part of every slavery

Doing what we do
      is only a small part of things

Love is the oxygen
    which keeps us alive
The spark inside of us
    is the sun that brings beauty and light and hope
Music is the voices within
    when words fail
Friends ~
    those who hold us upright
    when we no longer can stand

We need to know we're all in it together
Stop taking the oxygen out of the air we breathe
Get on your knees and pray
    for you have not stood for anything
    other than your private war within

But know this
I still have the spark
We can still get our hearts together
We will be complete
We are nothing
    but of each other

Dew drops will not discriminate
      which flower or leaf
      which color or branch
And when you look at the morning dew
      it is brilliantly beautiful

You took too long to paint a rose
It died

If you take too long to be awakened
You will die

It doesn't take time to end a life
It takes a lifetime to save a life

Brothers, sisters
    stop aiming at anyone's chest
Instead
Target their heart
    and shoot the old arrow of love
    deep in their heart

There is no effort in loving
It is only a great deep relief
    when your heart is freed
Why not then aim at the hearts
    of anyone who happens to be close by?
In other words
    love-by shooting

I want to learn no more
    about the affairs of men
I want to learn my connection
    to flowers, trees and watermelons
I want to ride rivers
    and visit new shores
I want to be lifted up by the highest waves of the ocean
    and lowered only by the sunsets
I want to join the world of
    non-language
    non-thinking
Just being

The more I am with the ocean
    the more real I become

A seagull becomes my teacher
    and pelican, a friend

I feel rich with life
    and sad with living

I think I am going to stay a little longer
    at the feet of this ocean

Be like grains of salt

Throw a pinch of you
     into a tasteless life

The grains of salt will vanish
     to bring a richness of taste to your soul

Be still

    and stillness . . . becomes . . . you

Be still

    till love moves you

Be still

    until you hear the warring voices disappear
    and peacefulness echoes from every corner of life

Live to see this

I cannot explain what is in your heart
    but I surely will feel it when you open

You are like a lamp ready to be lit
    and I am that torch to set you on fire

From there on
    it is your destiny to burn
    to the last fiber of your existence
    so that your final words to this world would be:

        I have loved enough

Come and celebrate
The broken wings have come home
We are together again

Never mind the difficulties
    of flying with broken wings
We are now in the healing mode
    and need not fly away to distances
        out of the reach of each other

Let the music begin
    For we are now flying within each other
        within each other . . .
            flying . . .

Love is a Spring breeze

You cannot capture it in your fist
You can feel it only when your hand is open

Watching the moon
I forgot that the ocean
    had been washing the sand around my feet
And I was more and more sinking

I looked down for a moment
    to save me from drowning
But the brightness of the moon
    would not release me

So I decided to sink
    into the beauty of the moon
And let go of worries
    about sinking into the ocean

There is more to life
    than worrying about sinking

The freshness of life begins
    when you give up your secrets

You breathe in newness
The freshness rises
    and stale being disappears

Then you begin to paint your present life
    with preciousness
Now you are really alive

I told my secret to a single tear
A fish drank it
    and told the ocean
Ocean told the clouds
Clouds told the rain
Rain told the earth
Earth gave birth to a rose
Rose told me
    'The secret you shared will always be a secret'

Everyone has a secret and needs to tell someone
Tell it to a rose
        an ocean
           a cloud
              the rain
                  or a tear

I am looking at the sunset
while dawn breaks in my heart

It is tricky business when you are in love

A darvish
Strolling in a rose garden
    sinking into the beauty of the garden
Not knowing
    stepped on a fallen rose

He saw what he had done
    knelt down and whispered
        'I am sorry'

The rose whispered back
    'Did you smell the fragrance of my life?'

The darvish said
    'It is that fragrance
        that brought me to this realization'

The flower said
    'Then, my friend
        my life's purpose has been served
        and our friendship is complete'

Work on your own story
    and tell it like a rose would
The essence and beauty of who you are
    is the only story

Stop compromising
You are not meant to be that way

God gave us flowers
    not to look at them
    but to be like them

So unfold your heart like a flower opening
    and send the essence of your being
    to everyone
        everywhere
    like a flower does
        every time
            always

A songbird
Morning breeze
And the sunrise
Grant you permission to a new day

Tell me
Who is the fool
      to wake up with a gloomy heart
            and suffer all day?

Can you put half of your heart into loving a flower
      and not the other half?

Can you open one eye
      and not see all?

Then once you say 'I love'
      you are loving all the way

Tonight
Let us taste devotion
    while it lasts

Whatever comes after
    will go down easier

Speak
    poetry

Laugh
    from where joy is made

Cry
    as though pearls are rolling off your face

Be sad
    only if you didn't love enough

Meet me after midnight
    when everyone has gone
        and quietness has spread its wings over the night
I will be waiting in the shadow of the night
    with a candle lit to guide you in

When you arrive
    we'll sit around the candle
Then I will put out the flame
Thereafter we shall use the light
    that is emitted from your face
    aimed at my heart

Our conversation will be short
    but it will take all night to complete
Then I will light up the candle once again
    to guide you out of the dark
    and you can return back home

The secret of our conversation
    shall be preserved in our hearts
None will be told
But wherever we go
    our secret will reveal itself
        by emitting light, love and acceptance
No words could explain
Our secret shall become the sacred
    to pass along for the next ones
        and the next ones

Dance near me
>	so I can feel motion

Talk with me
>	so I can drop the veils of deceit
>	>	and become pure

Hold me tight
>	so I can get to know how deeply
>	>	I long for my truth

Walk with me
>	so I can disappear into the future in peace

Like a drop of rain
    I fall to earth
        every time I hear you walking
Like birds
    I soar the skies
        every time I see you rising

This ocean of love
    has been drowning me toward you
        more and more

Take me with you

In your presence
I will be so light
      I could ride on your eyelash
      never to be noticed
      for I will see what you see

I will land in your thoughts
      for I will travel with the same wave as your thoughts

Finally
I will carry your heart in mine
      for there would be no life worth living
      without you

When love opens me up
    I can take in the whole universe

When love is gone
    I am so closed
    even my own life is squeezed out of me

Some doors are for walking out
Some doors are for walking in

And some doors are so wide open
    that there is no walking out or walking in
All are welcome and no one leaves

When I heard you coming
I ran to your nearest opening
    to greet you with my love

When you bowed before me and kissed the ground
I become the dirt that touched your lips

When you stood up and walked into me
I was that firmness beneath your feet
    that held you deep in my heart
        so we could see eye-to-eye
        and carry on a heart-to-heart conversation

All who know
Understand that
    infinity is immeasurable

But a Sufi says
You can taste infinity
    with a cup of love

A Sufi is a swan
      lifting off the surface of still water

A beautiful struggle to ascend
Then airborne
Then calm
Then the grace of the moment
Then no trace . . .

Only in silence
can you hear souls

And that is the poetry of love

A thousand eyes
  will not see any more of the moon
  than a single eye

One love story
  tells all

Love is a shock wave

that shakes every fiber
that weaves our existence

Let us be clear

to make love to everything we touch

As far as I am concerned
One breath of true love
      is worth a whole lifetime

That is the only reason I keep breathing

Lover is that one who hears you
then unveils you
to run naked
from flowering to flowering

An eternal blossoming

One night
The sky was so beautiful at full moon
    I did not know which one of us was higher
The moon or me

When you plant a seed of love
      it will grow deeply
Every leaf of the plant
      is a new breath
Every flower
      will give you a new beginning
Every branch
      becomes a new growth
And in its shadow
      friends gather for safety

And in the autumn
When the leaves fall
      they whisper on the way down

'I will see you next Spring
      with new life
      new growth
      and fresh breath
      in a new vibration
           that will make your music
                play you deeply
      and new shade
           shall invite fresh friends'

When you are gone in the morning
I will replace you with
      the biggest tear I can muster
Or place a rose where you sat
Maybe I will light up a candle
      to mimic your dancing flame
Or plant my heart where you stood
Or take a look at the stars to find you among them

And when it all ends
      I will find that nothing can replace you
And I will forever be grateful
      for the time you blessed me

Who knows what time will dictate to us
Maybe we can be together again

How can I walk away
>   when you are the strength of my feet?
How can I look away
>   when you are the sight of my eyes?
How can I speak of anything but poetry
>   when I speak of you?

Let us stop walking away
>   and looking any further
Sit with me and make poetry

You pull one strand
    my whole fabric falls
Then you touch me
    and I am together again

If you ever have to leave
    let me be the path you walk on

Poetry is a way of grooming a feeling
Nothing else

But if it grooms the people nearby
    then it is a revelation

God will be happier
	if you change your prayer
		to sweet love songs

Infinite knowledge
	knows every prayer there is to be made
	but will come to its knees
		for a sweet song
	and will dance to the heartbeat of a drummer

Be precise with your wink
	not your words

An ocean of love refuses no tear

Think of this for a moment
In the world of emotion
	all rivers are made from tears
	all dawns are out of awakening
	all sunsets are made from joy
	and all moonlight is made for lovemaking

There is a light within us
You must close your eyes to see it

That inner light
    guides you to see the purpose to live
The outer light
    lets you see where you stand
    and who is a friend

Walk with your heart
Look with your love
Touch with your soul

Take me in as a friend
Take my poison
    and turn it into a fountain of joy
Turn the true light of life into my living
Take what I have gone through
    and will it to forgiveness
Put dancing in my legs and wings into my arms
    and put your face in my future

For I gave up dying yesterday
And my new occupation is living
    for all lives
If you accept this offering
    sign in the bottom of that corner
    where no one else can touch
And seal it with a smile

It is about being beautiful
    and feeling preciousness
You do not love someone
Instead you share your loving being

In this world
    lover and Beloved are two separate things
But in the creation of things
    lover and Beloved are one

Practice revealing yourself
    like a rose

In my world
    veiling beauty is a cardinal sin

God created the darkness
    not to cover up
But to show the infinite stars of beauty
And to enhance every little flame of love

Gathering fragrant blossoms
is like finding new friends

The ones who will enhance your own fragrance

When will you know the truth?

When your heart is laughing

I love the wind
    that entangles your long hair
I love the fruit
    that resembles your taste
I love the rain
    when it touches my face
    like your tears washing my sins
I love the sunset
    which portrays your colorful face
I love the fragrance of flowers
    which puts me in touch with your breath
I love the birds
    that show me your ascending soul
I love the waterfalls
    which reveal the contours of your falling hair
        over your naked body

In short
I love all that exists
For your beauty is so vast
    that I see your resemblance
        in everything I see
            taste
                touch
                    or hear

I saw you today
    waving in concert with the waving ocean
I saw you riding on the back of seagulls
    and ascending with my heart

I felt you as you rained down on my face
Then your sunshining came through
    and chased the mist of rain away

You showed me how insignificant I was
    next to the sea
And how great I felt
    with the warmth of your sun

Yes
Definitely I saw you today
When tomorrow comes
    I will bring my friends to see you too

I am an ocean
I carry vastness
I become violently unstable
    with a tear
I move the sand to massage the tired feet
I send clouds with thunder and lightning
    to rekindle the old fire

If that is not enough
I will surrender to eternity
    to see you happy

At last
I found that I must make love to life itself
    not to suffer for it

At last
I realized that every kiss
    is a breath of God

At last
I know that I will never be separated from love
    no matter who rules

At last
    me
    laughter
    grace
    being generous and loving
Are all that are in this life

And the other life?
    Forget it
Doesn't exist . . . does not exist

I put you in my hand
    You move in my heart
I put you in my mind
    You give me light
I close my eyes to feel you
    You free my soul
I walk toward you
    You move the earth beneath me
I want to join with you
    You say it is not the time

I have never seen such beautiful conflict

This soul will disappear
    without the sound of your opening
As I near your opening
    I tremble with joy
When my heart consumes your perfume
    my tears will fall back
    and my smile covers the whole earth

Such reunion is not normal to humans
But it is an everyday event among gods
    where essence marries and remarries
        with flowing from heart to heart

A perfect opening
A perfect being
And finally . . .
A perfect non-being

Lately my friendships have been limited to
    those who love
      and those who don't love

Those who love
    are friends of everyone
And those who do not love
    need friends

When I am quiet
    I am not quiet
Lack of words
    does not mean the fire is out

In fact
When I'm alone at night without words
I shout to everyone everywhere
    to not let the fire go out

Let not the words
    do all the talking
Let not the kerosene lamp
    be all your light

No
I am not quiet
When I am quiet

The magic of love is
> to turn the evening
>> to shine like high noon
> to turn flame
>> to dance with your soul

The magic of love
> is to turn a kiss
>> into a lifetime of loving

The higher magic of love
To become invisible
> just a candle
>> which only shines for lovers

As the sun sets in the west
    and moon rises somewhere else
It is what we do
    that gives them brightness in our lives

Looked at the universe
    to discover what part I play
When I looked through my small eyes
    I saw infinite infinities

Then I realized
    that one small being can love infinitely
    and an infinite love can dignify the smallest being

With such a small heart
    such incredible love

With such small eyes
    greatest of visions

With small words
    an ocean of emotion

With a few simple notes
    world of music

What makes these possible?

Meet me at the crossroad of love
And I will show you how such small things
    make such incredible differences

Beneath my feet
    this dirt
That carries the secret
    of 13 billion years of changes

Above my head
    the sky
Over 100 billion light years of galaxies

And in my chest
    a heart with one love
That has the capacity
    to contain the dirt beneath my feet
    to the galaxies above my head

I can take you in with one breath
    and let you out with the next
Many suns have set
    since I have realized this love

For this love
    I will give up all the galaxies
With this love
    I will give up
    all realization, enlightenment and Samadhi

For without love
    nothing is worth anything
And with this love
    like the light of the sun and a match
    nothing else is measurable

In conclusion
Love is belonging

The only thing
that raises you beyond all imagination
is love

I was going homeward
    minding my own business
A rose from the side of the road yelled at me
    'Whoa, old man!
    Not so fast
    I wasn't put on the side of this road
        so you could run by me
    I am here to greet you
    The least you can do is slow down.
    You may never see another rose in your lifetime
    What would your life be worth then?'

My knees buckled
    and I knelt down to face the rose
We conversed . . . .

You have to admit
    it's quite a challenge to understand rose talk
One word from one petal
Another word from the next petal
And a golden heart in a deeper level
    spewing the essence of unbearable ecstasy

I was quite overwhelmed
    by so much contribution
        to the growth of my heart

I said to the rose
    'How could I leave you?'
The rose replied
    'Now that we have understood each other
        you could take me with you
    for my job on the side of this road is complete'

So I did
Picked up the rose by its stem
    and I know not how long we walked
All I know is
When I came to
    I became so conscious of relating
    to something so small in such a big way
        . . . I become a rose . . .
    to offer my life to people who come by to visit
    and take me with them

Until the next rose by the side of your path
    I bid you 'Fare well'

Do not ask my lips why I say such things
    Listen with your heart . . . and know

Do not look at my tears and ask why
    Drink my tears . . . and know

Do not ask why I have a need for a good day to die
    Look into my eyes . . . and know

Do not ask why I have been reduced to ashes
    Listen to my song . . . and know

Do not ask why I have left everything
    Raise your head
    Take in the stars . . . and know

Do not ask why I have become slave to a rose
    Kneel before a rose
    Smell its fragrance . . . to know

Those who call yourselves lovers
Know this
No love comes to you
    without the taste of morning dew
        on the face of a rose

Do not ask why I was in tears, came out laughing
    Understand . . . and know

Do not ask why I was dead, became alive
    Become love . . . and know

Keep arriving
    even when you do not move
        from place to place

Bring with you
    new feelings
    new thoughts
Constantly leave
    old thinking
    and old feeling

New vision
New birth
That is what 'arriving' means

Coming into a new space
    at the height of this newness
        there is another
Even death is an arriving place

Keep arriving
Keep arriving

When you come knocking and I am not there
    you are knocking at the wrong door
I reside in your heart

When you are lonely
    I am there to sing for you
When you are crying
    I catch your teardrops
    to grow roses with
When you are tired
    I put spring in your body
When you are sad
    I bring inspiration into your life

Come in
Sit by my side
    for I am your heart
        I am your heart

Finally
When you fall in love
    I dance on the lips of those you kiss
When you look for love
    I dance on your eyelashes
    to make you see the path of true love
And when you speak
    I bring music to your words

We will no longer do without each other
    Never . . .
        Never . . .

From a single cell
    I became a human

From a single heart
    I became a lover

From a single mind
    I became a creator

From a single smile
    I lost my control

From a single tear
    I trembled to my core

From a single soul
    I became the universe

Tell me
Am I just a name?
Am I this tired old body?
Am I this life with its infinite limitations?
Or am I none of these
    with infinite possibilities?

Who I am
>	is what separates us
Who I am not
>	will connect us

My insignificance
>	is not worthy of any recognition
What should be recognized
>	is our connection
Through the poetry that is within us
>	and among us

I may be old and crumbling
But at a right moment
    I could appear as a floating blossom
    as fresh as the day you fall in love

Like a migrating bird

my heart travels from friend to friend

A sunset is a promise that says
    'I will be back'

How can anyone forget
    the immense beauty of infinite color
        displayed with one single brush
            that keeps brushing
                until surrender to total darkness
            and yet says
                'I will be back'?

The day they created fire, earth and water
I became all of that

Yesterday I said 'Yes'
I became water
    to quench the thirst
I became fire
    to burn for love
And I became earth
    to bury the past

That is what 'becoming' means

You will never find me

If a tear drops by
      or a smile brushes your face
      or a song bursts out of your chest
You know I have come to visit

Those were the days
    when the only thing I ever stole
        was a kiss
    and the only word I spoke
        was my eye winking at you
    and the only promise you gave me
        was your smile

Those were the days that I still remember

Let me stay a little longer
You see
We have not finished holding hands by the sea
We did not tell all the stories to the seagulls
    chasing the waves and diving for fish

I remember
The promise we made
    to come back to the seaside
Watching the moon rising
    and hearing the song of it coming up every night
        just to shine on us

Let me stay a little longer
The walk on the shore of the seven seas
    is not complete
What about the sun rising
    hosting the first light
    warming our hearts
    and giving us the taste of ecstasy
    and the promise of joy of life?

We haven't begun to climb every mountain
    and stroll every river
Snow, spring, summer and fall
Who would it harm
    if you grant the wishes of an old man on his way out?
Please let me stay a little longer

And when the end comes
    I will shout out loud
'I have seen it all
    and done everything there was to do'
And say
'Wow! It was beautiful . . . and it's time to go'

Who knows where the time goes

I remember the time
    when the stars were bright
    and I could touch them

I remember in my total darkness
    a full moon came up
    just to touch my heart

Where has the time gone?

The stars will always be there
So will the full moon
But the time will come
    when I will not be there

Now is the time
    to finish all my hellos and good-byes
Will never forget
    the paths I have traveled
    and roses I have met

Who knows where these times go?

I promise to fulfill all the times
    that have been set before me

Till that time
    I will love you

If there is anything to be
be love

www.ingramcontent.com/pod-product-compliance
Lightning Source LLC
Chambersburg PA
CBHW052028070526
44584CB00016B/1947